daylight for Women
leader's guide

D1232813

Red
Hot
Faith

Lessons from a Lukewarm Church

daylight *for* Women

leader's guide

Red Hot Faith

Lessons from a Lukewarm Church

8 Group Bible Study Sessions for Women

Featuring Cindy Bultema

DISCOVERY HOUSE
PUBLISHERS®

Feeding the Soul with the Word of God

The Daylight for Women Bible Studies video was produced by *Day of Discovery*, a Bible-teaching TV series of RBC Ministries.

Red Hot Faith was taped on location in Grand Rapids, Michigan, and in Turkey

© 2014 by Discovery House Publishers

Discovery House Publishers is affiliated with RBC Ministries, Grand Rapids, Michigan.

Requests for permission to quote from this book should be directed to:
Permissions Department
Discovery House Publishers
P.O. Box 3566
Grand Rapids, MI 49501
Or contact us by e-mail at permissionsdept@dhp.org

Interior design by Sherri L. Hoffman
Cover design by Jeremy Culp
Cover photo by iStockphoto

ISBN: 978-1-57293-778-9

Printed in the United States of America
First Printing 2014

Contents

A Note from Cindy

I'll never forget the first time I led a women's Bible study. My girlfriend Julie prayerfully decided we should start a Tuesday night study in her home, and I should facilitate it. I did not feel the same way. Who was I to lead a Bible study? What if no one showed up? Or worse—what if a large number came the first week, and then no one came back? Lead a group for women? No way!

I did, however, promise Julie that before I gave my final answer, I would pray. As I sought God, something unexpected happened. Slowly but surely my fears began fading away. As I searched the Scriptures, I was reminded that God wasn't looking for perfect people, just simple servants. Was I willing to be prayerful, prepared, and open to His leading? I asked God to increase my faith and humbly said, "Yes."

Before long, our group outgrew Julie's home, and we had to move to a church building. We continued to meet and expand, and five years later, I wrote some lessons called *Red Hot Faith* to share with this flourishing gathering. The rest, they say, is history. God has accomplished more than we ever imagined possible.

Sweet friend, I don't know if this is your first time facilitating a women's Bible study or your fiftieth. But I do know this: God is still in the business of looking for imperfect women—just like me, just like you—whose hearts are fully committed to Him, women He can use for His kingdom purposes.

My hope is that you find the *Red Hot Faith* curriculum to be a helpful tool as you gather women to dig into God's Word together so they can learn and grow. This Leader's Guide was created to assist and support you every step of the way. Not only is it filled with helpful tips, suggestions, activities, and handouts, but it also provides some wise words of encouragement written by women's leaders from all across the United States.

I trust that their messages will remind you that there is an army of women cheering for you on this *Red Hot Faith* journey. Also, feel free to contact me any time for prayer and assistance. You are not alone!

May God bless you, my dear sister, and empower and equip you with everything you need as you begin your *Red Hot Faith* adventure.

Sweet blessings,

Cindy

How to Use the Leader's Guide

Red Hot Faith: Lessons from a Lukewarm Church is a video and discussion-based Bible study. During the eight sessions, women will delve into the book of Revelation, where we hear Jesus' words to the church of Laodicea—a church reprimanded for its lukewarm faith. Please don't let the book of Revelation intimidate you. Whether your group members have been studying the Bible for decades or are still trying to figure out this "Jesus thing," you'll find relevant materials that meet women right where they are on their spiritual journey. For some, the concepts will be new and intriguing; for others, they will be strengthening and confirming.

The goal of the *Red Hot Faith Leader's Guide* is to equip you with tips, tools, and techniques that can help you effectively and prayerfully plan for your weekly gatherings. You'll find icebreakers, group activities, prayer prompts, handouts, detailed session overviews, as well as step-by-step instructions for facilitating your group sessions. Also, go to www.cindybultema.com for additional information, video testimonies, and other resources.

To prepare for a positive small-group experience, please read the following information before beginning.

Group Size

The *Red Hot Faith* curriculum is best experienced in a group setting such as a neighborhood Bible study, Sunday school class, office lunch hour get-together, or other small-group gathering. After the members view the video teaching together, they can then participate in a group discussion. Ideally, discussion groups should be no larger than eight to ten people. If your group is larger, you may want to watch the video together, and then break into smaller groups to encourage sharing from everyone.

Format

Red Hot Faith can be used by groups that meet for any length of time from one to two hours. As the facilitator, you decide the format that will work best with your gathering. Don't worry if your group only has an hour, you will still get to do all of the sections. You won't miss a thing!

Here is a sample breakdown based on different group times.

❨ 60-minute Group	❨❨ 90-minute Group	❨❨❨ 120-minute Group
Get Into It (10 minutes) • Welcome • Prayer • Icebreaker	**Get Into It** (15 minutes) • Welcome • Prayer • Icebreaker	**Get Into It** (20 minutes) • Welcome • Prayer • Icebreaker
Watch It (30 minutes) Video Teaching	**Watch It** (30 minutes) Video Teaching	**Watch It** (30 minutes) Video Teaching
Discuss It (15 minutes)	**Discuss It** (35 minutes)	**Discuss It** (40 minutes)
Wrap It Up (5 minutes) • Closing Prayer	**Wrap It Up** (10 minutes) • Closing Prayer	**Prayer Groups** (20 minutes)
		Wrap It Up (10 minutes) • Closing Prayer

Note: Questions and activities will be provided based on the different time formats. To make it "leader friendly," you'll notice choices differentiated with chili peppers throughout the Leader's Guide.

❨ If you are a 60-minute group, you may want to select the "one pepper" activities.

❨❨ If you are a 90-minute group, you may want to select the "two pepper" activities.

❨❨❨ If you are 2-hour group, you may want to select the "three pepper" activities.

Not One Size Fits All

The *Red Hot Faith* curriculum is a tool, but the ultimate goal is helping women grow closer to Jesus in the context of a welcoming and safe environment. For that reason, *Red Hot Faith* is designed to be informative, yet adaptable. If yours is a brand-new group, you may want more time in the beginning to get to know each other. If yours is an established group, you may want to complete the additional "three pepper" activities. If the women in your group are new to God's Word, you may want extra time examining the Scriptures. As the facilitator, shape the study to what best suits the needs and desires of your individual group.

Group Preparation

There may be more questions and activities provided than time may allow. That's okay! Before you gather, highlight the questions you want to emphasize during the session. Choose the questions best matched to the personal needs of your group. Do not feel that you have to ask every question. If there are discussion questions you are unable to cover, encourage the women to complete them during their personal Work On It time at home.

Session Summary

In the Leader's Guide, each session includes the following components.

Overview: A brief summary of the weekly lesson. This is not included in the Participant's Guide.

Prepare For It: Activities and planning tips you will want to consider and complete before your weekly group gathering.

Get Into It: An introduction to the session's theme, a choice of icebreaker questions, plus opening prayer reminders.

Watch It: An outline of the session's video teaching for group members to follow along and take notes if they wish.

Discuss It: Scripture passages to discuss. Questions that reinforce the session content and encourage personal input from every group member. Activities to support the session theme. Closing prayer ideas.

Work On It: "Homework" to enhance the video teachings while encouraging personal study, reflection, and application. Setting aside 60 to 90 minutes during the week (either all at one time or spread out during the week) will enable the women to complete the Work On It section.

Reflect On It: Thoughts to help you evaluate effectiveness after your group is over. Follow-up suggestions before your next gathering.

Scripture Memory

During each of the eight video teachings, a new Scripture memory verse ("Memorize It!") will be introduced. Encourage the women to renew their minds by memorizing the verses. Remind them to either (a) photocopy the verses located at the back of their Participant's Guide or (b) write the verses on index cards each week.

Know Your Group

One of the greatest ways you can prepare is to spend time "standing in the shoes" of your individual group members. Before your first gathering, devote time to prayerfully reflect on the following questions:

- Have the women been in small groups before? Is anyone brand-new to Bible study?
- Are the women Christians? Non-Christians? Not sure?
- How familiar is each woman with the Bible?
- How comfortable is each woman with prayer?
- What are the current challenges facing the women (busyness, loneliness, marriage struggles, aging parents, young children, etc.)

Ask God to give you discernment and extra sensitivity to the hearts of each woman in your group.

Just for Fun

The *Red Hot Faith* curriculum provides many opportunities to celebrate women as they step out of their comfort zones and put their faith into action. You may want to have a small "treasure chest" of fun incentives to support women on their *Red Hot Faith* adventure. Suggestions include the following: mini boxes of Red Hots™ candies, small votive candles (for being a light in the world), water bottles (for sharing a "cup of cold water" with others), or hot chocolate packets (for being "hot" on their "trade route"). The options are endless.

red hot tip

Don't forget to look for facilitating tips and personal notes sprinkled throughout this Leader's Guide to support and encourage you as you lead your *Red Hot Faith* group.

How to Create a Red Hot Faith Group

1. **Pray!** Ask God for guidance, direction, and wisdom for all of the planning details. You may want to create a prayer notebook to record your requests and note how God answers your prayers. Ask God to

   - Order your steps and lead you every step of the way
   - Handpick the women He wants to attend, and open each woman's mind and heart to the invitation
   - Ignite a sizzling faith-life for all who will be participating

2. **Choose your Bible study meeting dates.** Determine the number of weeks you would like to get together, and mark your calendar. Make sure holidays, school breaks, etc. won't interfere with your gatherings. (Note: you may want to plan a *Red Hot Faith* Fiesta as a ninth session. See page 50 [Leader's Guide, LG] for more details.)

3. **Determine your meeting location.** If you'll be gathering at a church or office, reserve a meeting room(s), a TV, and a DVD player.

4. **Enlist help from others.** Is there someone who might help with hospitality? Prayer? Snacks? Additional small-group leaders? Child care (if needed)?

   Remember: there is nothing like responsibility to help others feel valued.

5. **Prepare your invitation list.** Be brave and prayerfully think outside the box.

   Women to consider inviting to your group

   - Neighbors
   - Co-workers
   - Relatives
   - Friends
   - Teachers
   - Sports team parents
   - Exercise class members
   - School moms
   - Women you encounter on a day-to-day basis (store clerks, hair stylists, baristas, gym trainers, child-care workers, dental hygienists).

red hot tip

"If a name comes to mind while you are making your invitation list, don't dismiss it. It could be a prompt from the Holy Spirit. Maybe that woman's mom has been praying for someone to invite her daughter to a small group." —*Mary Swierenga, Grand Rapids, MI*

6. **Gather all your needed resources.** In addition to a TV and a DVD player, you'll need:

   - *Red Hot Faith* DVD
   - Participant's Guide (one per woman)
   - Bible (one per woman)
   - Leader's Guide (you may want one per small group leader)
   - Pens or pencils for all
   - Nametags, if appropriate
   - Index cards, paper, and/or poster board for some of the group activities

7. **Begin sharing publicly about your group** four weeks before the first session. Suggestions include sending e-mails, making phone calls, personally inviting neighbors, creating an Evite, or sharing on social media. Ask women to pre-register so you can plan accordingly.

red hot tip

"Don't be disappointed if your neighbors don't respond as you'd hoped, and don't be overwhelmed if more people come than you expected. As long as you are acting in obedience to God's direction, this is in His capable hands. Yes, God can count!"[1]
—*Amy Lively, Lancaster, Ohio*

8. **Create a "welcome" letter/packet** to distribute and discuss during the first session. Items you may want to include are the following: Overview of the group, values, schedule, and random "housekeeping" items. See page 54 (LG) as a sample.

9. **Get ready for the first gathering.** Use the Leader's Guide to help you successfully pray, plan, and prepare for Session 1.

10. **Send reminder e-mails or make phone calls** to your *Red Hot Faith* group members the day before your first session.

11. **Keep praying and have fun!**

red hot tip

"Dear Facilitator, Ask someone to be your prayer partner and to pray for you as you lead your *Red Hot Faith* study. Do you know someone who would do that? An elderly person? A friend from another town? Give that friend a ministry and a way to be a part of it, even if she can't be there in person. I pray that all the *Red Hot Faith* facilitators have a 'prayer warrior' in their corner as they lead each week."

—*April Garretson, Christiansburg, Virginia*

10 Tips to "Be-Ing" an Effective Facilitator

1. **Be rooted.** Remain in the Lord, and remember that you can't do anything apart from Him (John 15:5). Carve out plenty of time in your daily schedule to spend with the Lord in prayer, solitude, and Bible reading.[2]

2. **Be prepared.** Read through the suggested discussion questions and activities. Before each meeting, select the options that will work best for your group. Gather any handouts and resources you'll need.

3. **Be flexible.** There may be times you'll need to surrender your carefully prepared plan and proceed in a completely different direction. Be perceptive to the needs of the women, and be adaptable when needed.

4. **Be authentic and transparent.** It is amazing how others will open up when the leader is real and speaking from her heart. Your leadership will set the tone for the group.

5. **Be timely.** A good rule of thumb: Always start on time and end on time.

6. **Be prayerful.** Pray about every aspect of your group. Ask God for His help and leading, and pray for your group members by name. When you pray, you gain access to God's supernatural power. "Pray continually" (1 Thessalonians 5:17).

7. **Be grace-filled.** Ask God to infuse you with His grace each week. Did someone forget her Participant's Guide? Extend grace. Not complete her homework? Give more grace. Model care and compassion rather than rules and regulations.

8. **Be the facilitator.** A teacher is the only one teaching, but a facilitator encourages the group to share, gently draws people out, asks questions to get a good discussion going, and keeps track of the time and schedule.

9. **Be sensitive.** Pay attention to the physical, emotional, or spiritual needs of each participant. If you are concerned about the overall well-being of any of the women, encourage them to seek counseling and/or professional help.

10. **Be YOU!** If you like decorations and themes, be creative and play along with the weekly ideas. If you enjoy whipping up spicy dishes, cook away. Please don't worry about completing all the activities. Allow your unique personality and perspective to shine through. Be a first-class YOU as a facilitator!

red hot tip

....

"As you prepare to lead this study, spend some time letting go of your expectations and ask God to show you how He wishes to move in your group. God has a plan and His is best."

—*Jennifer Ferguson, Austin, Texas*

....

SESSION 1

The Journey Begins

Overview: The first group session! The hope is to create a welcoming, safe, and authentic environment for the women to learn more about the *Red Hot Faith* study, its author, and most important, God's unfailing, unconditional love.

Prepare For It

Things to do before the session

- Review the time formats on page 9 (LG). Decide on a schedule for your gathering. Read the Get Into It and Discuss It sections in your Participant's Guide and select the questions that will work best for your group.

- Watch Session 1 to familiarize yourself with Cindy's story.

- Confirm you have all materials needed (see page 13 LG).

- Handouts: Welcome handout/packet, if desired. Also, for an additional icebreaker, copy the *Red Hot Faith* Icebreaker on page 55 (LG). Make one handout per woman.

- Snacks: Decide if you'd like to offer refreshments, but don't feel obligated. One easy solution: tortilla chips, salsa, and something sweet (chocolate works great). Keep it simple.

- Pray specifically for God to remove any obstacles that would hinder the women from attending, and ask Him to infuse you with His love, joy, wisdom, and perfect peace.

red hot tip

Welcome!

As the women arrive, greet each one with a warm welcome. Help each woman get comfortable as she signs in, fills out a name tag, and grabs any needed supplies (Participant's Guide, pen, handouts) and refreshments.

Get Into It

- Welcome everyone to *Red Hot Faith* and open with a brief prayer.
- Introduce yourself and share your hopes for your *Red Hot Faith* group. Introduce other leaders as appropriate.
- Get to know each another. Choose one of the questions from the Breaking the Ice exercises on page 18 of the Participant's Guide (PG).
- Distribute the *Red Hot Faith* Icebreaker from page 55 (LG). Give everyone three minutes to complete as much as they can on the handout. In groups of four to six participants, go through the questions and share your answers together.

    Note: Be sure that no one feels pressure to answer the questions. Be sensitive to those who may be quiet/shy, especially since it's the first group gathering. For some, it may have been a stretch to even attend the study.

- Share your Welcome packet and/or any Red Hot Faith details with your group. You may want to include the following:
    - Schedule for the next seven to eight weeks
    - Group values (confidentiality, authenticity, etc.)

- Overview of the *Red Hot Faith* study (30-minute video teachings, weekly memory verse opportunity, homework)
- Miscellaneous items such as snack schedule or cell phone etiquette.

● Pass around paper and ask everyone to record her name, e-mail address, and phone number. Type up a Small Group Directory and distribute it next week.

● Have everyone open to page 18 of her Participant's Guide. Read the "Road Trip!" introduction from Cindy.

Watch It

Direct everyone to Watch It on page 19 (PG). Show the Session 1 video: "The Journey Begins."

Discuss It

● Facilitate the Discuss It questions beginning on page 21 (PG).

● Memory Verse: Facilitator, do you have a story of how Scripture memory has affected you? Share with the women, and remind them of the goal to memorize eight new verses together.

● Prayer Time: Read the note from Cindy regarding prayer on page 24 (PG). Has anyone else ever felt that way? Encourage the women to use the prayer prompts to pray for each other during the coming week. Close in prayer.

(((● Prayer Groups: Break into groups of four. Invite the women to pray for one another using the prayer prompts on page 24 (PG). Remind the women that it is okay to "take a pass" on praying out loud if they'd prefer.

Work On It

Direct the women to the "spiritual thermometer" on page 25 (PG). They won't want to miss taking their current spiritual temperature at home this week. Also, remind them to carve out time to complete the brief Work On It section before your next gathering.

spice it up

Don't forget to take a quick "before" photo of your group and e-mail it to cindy@cindybultema.com.

red hot tip

"Spend a few minutes after your last guest leaves to recap your gathering. You won't regret doing it now, but you *will* forget if you do it later."[3] —*Amy Lively, Lancaster, Ohio*

Reflect On It

A self-review of your time after the session

- How did it go? What were two things that went really well?
- Is there anything you wish you had done differently?
- Spend time in prayer thanking God for His guidance and asking Him to continue to lead you every step of the way. Pray that the women will carve out time to open the Word and complete their Work On It activities this week.
- Is there anyone who needs a special word of encouragement? Mail a note, send an e-mail, or make a quick phone call.

red hot tip

"Just between us: The first week always seems the worst! In spite of all the preparation, I know you had a few surprises today. Rather than dwelling on the minor complications, think instead of the major completions God will do during these Bible study sessions. I pray you feel His lavish love in your life every single day."[4] —*Beth Moore*

Letter to the Lukewarm

Overview: Unpack the startling truths found in Revelation 3:14–22, the letter to the church of Laodicea. We'll define significant themes such as red hot, lukewarm, and repentance, as well as reflect on our personal faith relationship with Jesus.

Prepare For It

Things to do before the session

- Review your schedule based on your time frame (see page 9 LG for help). Read through the Get Into It and Discuss It sections of your Participant's Guide and note which questions will work best for your group.

- Watch Session 2 to familiarize yourself with the teaching.

  Note: During the video, Cindy asks the questions, "Have you opened the door to Jesus? Have you asked Jesus to be the Lord and Savior of your life?" Are you comfortable sharing the gospel? If not, you may want to read through Work On It No. 3 on page 43 (PG) to help you communicate how to "open the door" to Jesus.

- Handouts: Prepare and distribute a Small Group Directory to help the woman to stay connected.

- Pray for each woman by name. Ask God to prepare her heart for this significant teaching, remove unbelief, and infuse her with fresh faith. Also, pray for an atmosphere where each woman feels safe—physically, emotionally, and spiritually.

● Send a reminder e-mail and let all of the women know you are looking forward to seeing them soon!

red hot tip

....

"It may only be week two, but God is already at work in your group. I'll never forget the time God brought an unregistered, unexpected, unknown, ungodly woman to our gathering during week two. She only came once, but it was the day we shared the gospel, and her honest questions moved the hearts of every woman in the room. Expect God to do great things, and record them as they unfold!"
—*Julie Sanders, Knoxville, Tennessee*

....

Get Into It

● Welcome everyone and open with prayer.

● Communicate any updates with your group. You may want to include the following:
- Schedule for the next seven to eight weeks
- Review of the group values (confidentiality, authenticity, etc.)
- Miscellaneous, such as snack schedule, cell phone etiquette
- Distribute the Small Group Directory

(● Choose one of the Breaking the Ice exercises on page 30 (PG).

((● To help remember each other's names, have the women introduce themselves using a positive adjective that starts with the first letter of their first name. (i.e. Lovable Laurie, Amazing Amelia, Helpful Heather.)

(((● After completing one of the Breaking the Ice exercises, review the "spiritual thermometer" from page 25 (PG). Have each woman share one idea that would help increase her spiritual temperature.

● Have everyone open to page 30 of her Participant's Guide. Read the "First, the Bad News" introduction from Cindy.

Watch It

Direct everyone to Watch It on page 31 (PG). Play the Session 2 video: "Letter to the Lukewarm."

Discuss It

- Facilitate the Discuss It questions beginning on page 35 (PG).
- Do you have "seekers" in your group? Turn to No. 3 in the Work On It section (p. 43 PG) and read it aloud slowly, pausing to invite questions, as needed. Ask, "If you have not made this life-changing decision, would you prayerfully consider doing so now?"

((● Memory Verse (p. 34 PG): Does anyone have a favorite Scripture memory tip?

Share your ideas, and encourage the group to memorize this week's verse.

Facilitator, if you don't have a favorite tip, you might encourage the women to write the verse on their bathroom mirror at home with a dry erase marker.

(((● Memory Verse: Pass out paper/index cards. Have each woman write out this week's verse. Suggest keeping it on the car dashboard and saying it aloud while driving.

- Prayer Time: Encourage the women to use the prayer prompts to pray for each other during the coming week. Ask for a volunteer to close in prayer.

(((● Prayer Groups: Break into groups of four. Encourage the women to share one of their responses to what would help increase their spiritual temperature on page 25 (PG). With this information, pray for one another. Remind the women that it is okay to "take a pass" on praying out loud if they'd prefer.

Work On It

Encourage the women to take time to complete the Work On It section at home. Draw attention to the Lukewarm Checklist (p. 38 PG) and urge them to complete the "check-up" during the week.

red hot tip

"Remember, you don't have to be an expert to be used by God. You don't have to know all the answers to lead a group of women. Don't be afraid to be authentic and vulnerable. Trust in God's strength to accomplish your leadership tasks." —*Sharla Fritz, Chicago, Illinois*

Reflect On It

A self-review of your time after the session

- How did it go? Is there anything you wish you had done differently?
- What worked well? Can you name five things?
- Think about the different learning styles—visual, auditory, reading/writing, and kinesthetic. Are you able to incorporate all four learning styles into your small-group setting? Is there something new you could try next week to ensure that you are connecting with all the group members in a way that is helpful to them?
- Spend time in prayer. Ask God to reveal to each woman any areas of life where she needs to "open the door" to Jesus.
- Call or write group members who were absent. Let them know they were missed.

red hot tip

"Do not be afraid of silence in the group. This is an indication that the women are thinking deeply on your question. To keep your mind busy, count to about 15; if there is no response by then, ask the question in a different way or ask, 'Has anyone come up with anything?' "
—*Kathy Bruins, Holland, Michigan*

SESSION 3

Be of Some Use

Overview: "Be hot! Be cold! Be something!" This phrase will soon be crystal clear after our visit to Laodicea, as well as the neighboring cities of Hierapolis and Colosse. We'll be reminded how difficult it is to live contentedly (especially when we compare ourselves to others) and how God desires to use His church members to make an impact on their personal "trade routes."

Prepare For It

Things to do before the session

- Read the Get Into It and Discuss It sections in your Participant's Guide and choose the questions that will work best for your group.

- Preview Session 3 to familiarize yourself with the teaching, if possible.

- Optional Handouts: Trade Route take-home (page 60 LG).

- Trade Route: If possible, use Cindy's trade route as a guide to make your own. The women will enjoy seeing your personal artwork.

- Refreshments: Serve ice-cold water and steaming hot drinks—nothing lukewarm!

- Pray for each woman by name, asking God to open her eyes, ears, and heart to all that He wants to accomplish through the *Red Hot Faith* study.

red hot tip

Get Into It

- Welcome everyone and open with prayer.

- (Choose one of the Breaking the Ice exercises on page 46 (PG).

- ((Have a volunteer read aloud Romans 10:17 (Week 2 memory verse). Did anyone memorize it? How has the Scripture touched your life over the past week?

- (((After completing one of the Breaking the Ice exercises, divide the women into pairs. Ask participants to talk with a partner for 2 to 3 minutes on what they learned about Laodicea from last week. How is your city like Laodicea? How is it different? Option: Have some of the ladies share with the larger group what they learned after this time together. Remember, the more we learn about Laodicea, the more Christ's letter comes alive!

- Have everyone open to page 46 of her Participant's Guide. Ask a volunteer to read the "Useless" introduction by Cindy.

Watch It

Direct everyone to Watch It on page 47 (PG). Play the Session 3 video: "Be of Some Use."

Discuss It

- Facilitate the Discuss It questions beginning on page 51 (PG).

-)) Pass out a 3x5 card to each member of the group. Have each woman write "be hot, be cold, be of some use" on the notecard. On the flip side have them prayerfully reflect and then write one way they are going to "be of some use" this week. Suggest they put this notecard some place where they will see it throughout the week (bathroom mirror, dashboard of the car, near the computer, above the kitchen sink). Bring the card back next week and give an update.

-))) For Discuss It No. 6. on page 53 (PG), divide the women into groups of 3 to 4. Give each group a piece of paper. Give them five minutes to brainstorm ways to "be hot" or "be cold" on their trade route. Come back together and share the responses, creating one big master list filled with ideas.

- Memory Verse (p. 50 PG): Have a volunteer look up this week's memory verse: Colossians 3:23. Ask, "How can you apply this verse to your trade route this week?"

- Prayer Time: Encourage the women to use the prayer prompts to pray for each other during the coming week. Ask for a volunteer to close in prayer.

-))) Prayer Groups: Break into groups of four. Review what you learned about repentance last week (see page 36 in Participant's Guide for recap). Spend time together in prayer repenting for the ways you compare yourselves with others. Ask God to help you choose contentment over comparisons.

Work On It

Encourage the women to take time to complete the Work On It section at home, especially suggesting that each creates her own "trade route" on page 59 (PG). Share your personal example (or Cindy's) to get their creative juices flowing. You may want to offer a fun "incentive" for anyone bringing in a completed trade route (see page 11 in Leader's Guide for ideas).

red hot tip

"Week three marks a time when you are seeing some real commitment in your group. Recognize and encourage those who are staying the course. Ask God for specific ways to light a fire within your sisters who are falling behind and losing their vision."[5] *—Beth Moore*

Reflect On It

A self-review of your time after the session

- How did it go? Is there anything you wish you had done differently?
- What worked well?
- Spend time in prayer. Ask God to give each woman eyes to see where He might want to use her on her "trade route."
- Call or write group members who were absent. Check in to make sure they are okay, and see if there's anything the group can do to help.
- Would your group work well to do a service project together? Prayerfully consider coming together to "be hot" or "be cold" as a group. Ideas include serving at a soup kitchen, cleaning a church nursery, adopting a single mom, volunteering at a pregnancy resource center, and/or sending notes of encouragement to students. The ideas are endless!

red hot tip

"Got one in your group who wants to answer ALL the questions? Dominates the group? Call her during the week and ask her to help you with a project: Tell her that you have noticed that a few very quiet people need some silent moments before they will step into the quiet with their answers. Would she be willing to help create some of those moments? And would she pray with you for others to have courage in sharing? And don't forget to thank her when the project works!"
—Ginger Sisson, Grand Rapids, Michigan

SESSION 4

In Need of Nothing

Overview: The church members of Laodicea assumed that because they looked good "on the outside" everything was okay "on the inside." Big mistake. In this session, we'll discuss how to live from the inside out, rather than the outside in.

Prepare For It

Things to do before the session

- Read the Get Into It and Discuss It sections and choose the questions that will work best for your group.
- Watch Session 4 to familiarize yourself with the teaching.
- Handouts: Your "trade route."
- Optional Props: You may want to have three vases to reenact Cindy's vase demonstration, plus "random" items to place in the first two vases and a pitcher filled with water for the third.
- Pray that each group member will identify areas of self-reliance and turn to Christ for His sufficiency.

red hot tip

"A smile, a heartfelt hug, or a genuine compliment. These might be more inspirational to someone today than the lesson you have studied and prepared to lead today. Let God shine through you."

—*Lori Crispin, Boca Raton, Florida*

Get Into It

- ● Welcome everyone and open with prayer.
- ❨ ● Choose one of the Breaking the Ice exercises on page 63 (PG).
- ❨❨ ● Did anyone complete her "trade route" take-home exercise (p. 59 PG)? Share your artwork and/or your experiences about being hot and cold. Facilitator, have a personal "trade route" story to share to get the conversation started, if needed.
- ● Have everyone open to page 62 of her Participant's Guide. Ask a volunteer to read the "Looking Good? Maybe Not" introduction from Cindy.
- ❨❨❨ ● Share, "Cindy assumed since her friend looked good on the outside, everything must be good 'on the inside' too. How have you made a similar mistake?"

Watch It

Direct everyone to "Watch It" on page 64 (PG). Show the Session 4 video: "In Need of Nothing."

Discuss It

- Facilitate the Discuss It questions beginning on page 67.

((- Recreate the vase illustration as you go through the Discuss It question No. 4 on page 68 in the Participant's Guide.

- Memory Verse (p. 66 PG): Say to the women, "If you've fallen behind on memorizing, this is a perfect week to jump right back in." Ask for a show of hands for those women who commit to memorizing this week's verse.

(((- Memory Verse (p. 66 PG): Take a few moments and review the verses learned so far (1 John 3:1, Romans 10:17, and Colossians 3:23).

- Prayer Time: Using the prayer prompts as a guide, ask for a volunteer to close in prayer.

(((- Prayer Groups: Break into groups of two to four. Encourage each woman to write on a piece of paper the personal ways she turns to "outside things," and then trade the paper with someone else. With this information, pray for one another using Cindy's three-part recipe—come to Christ, let go, receive Christ's remedy—as a guide. Remind the women that it is okay to "take a pass" on praying out loud.

Work On It

Encourage the women to take time to complete the Work On It section at home. Also, remind them to be on the lookout for ways to be "hot" and "cold" on their trade route, and be ready to share with the group how they were "of some use."

spice it up

For extra fun, encourage the women to wear GOLD to group next week. Offer a prize for the most golden group member.

red hot tip

"Maybe you have noticed a member of your group who doesn't share as much as others or seems to be struggling with something. Think about whether a phone call or short note might help encourage her this week!" —Laura Kuperus, Grand Rapids, Michigan

Reflect On It

A self-review of your time after the session

- How did it go? What were the Top 3 things that worked well?
- Is there anything you wish you had done differently?
- Spend time in prayer. Ask that God would spur the women on toward obedience and real-life application.
- Call or write group members who were absent. Let them know they were missed. If it's been a week or two, let them know it's not too late to jump back in and see the study through to completion.
- Did you hear fun stories about how your group members are putting their Red Hot Faith into action? E-mail cindy@cindybultema.com, and you might be featured on Cindy's website: www.cindybultema.com

red hot tip

"I have to remember that I am the facilitator, not a pastor or theological student, and it is okay to simply say, 'I don't know' if the conversation turns to an area where I'm clueless." —Andrea Sellers, Dale, Texas

SESSION 5

Testing Times

Overview: A woman with Red Hot Faith withstands the heat of the tests and trials that come her way. Journey to "Master Goldsmith" Ayhan Usta's goldsmith shop to discover how the "refiner's fire" can help shape and mold our faith and not destroy it.

Prepare For It

Things to do before the session

- 🔴 Read the Get Into It and Discuss It sections and choose the questions that will work best for your group.
- 🔴 Watch Session 5 to familiarize yourself with the teaching.
- 🔴 Handouts: The blank "God's Attributes from A to Z" on page 56 (LG).
- 🔴 Ask God to give you wisdom and understanding as you prepare for a lesson that could bring up painful thoughts, experiences, and emotions. Pray for each woman by name and by need.
- 🔴 Send an encouraging e-mail and remind the women to wear GOLD to group. Have your camera ready!

red hot tip

Get Into It

● Welcome everyone and open with prayer.

❨ ● Choose one of the Breaking the Ice exercises on page 79 (PG).

❨❨ ● Has anyone had a chance to be "hot" or be "cold" on her trade route? Share your experiences about being hot and cold. Facilitator, have a personal "trade route" story to share to get the conversation started, if needed.

❨❨❨ ● Review the list of Christ's remedies on page 75 (PG). Go around the room and read each statement aloud (i.e. To the weary, Jesus extends rest . . .). Ask, "Which reminder do you most need to hear today? Explain as you feel comfortable."

● Have everyone open to page 78 of her Participant's Guide. Read "The Refiner's Fire" introduction from Cindy.

Watch It

Direct everyone to Watch It on page 80 (PG). Show the Session 5 video: "Testing Times."

Discuss It

- Facilitate the Discuss It questions beginning on page 84 (PG).

)) - Have a volunteer read aloud the "five lessons from trials" shared in the video (pp. 81–82 PG). Ask, "How have you experienced one of these lessons firsthand?" Facilitator, have a story to share if needed to get the conversation started.

))) - Invite a volunteer to read aloud Hebrews 12:3–11. Discuss, How does it encourage you to know that times of testing prove that we, as believers, are God's dearly loved children, whom He wants to grow in faith and to trust Him? What if we looked at discipline as an opportunity for "train-ing" in righteousness and peace? How could this change of perspective help us when going through the fire?

- Memory Verse (p. 83 PG): Have each woman write out the verse on paper or an index card. Encourage her to keep it close, and say it aloud often.

- Prayer Time: Encourage the women to use the prayer prompts to pray for each other during the coming week. Ask for a volunteer to close in prayer.

))) - Prayer Groups: Break into groups of four. Spend time praying for women who are going through seasons of testing and trial. Ask God to strengthen their faith, and reveal himself to them in tangible ways. Remind the women that it is okay to "take a pass" on praying out loud.

Work On It

Pass out the blank "God's Attributes from A to Z" handout (p. 56 LG). Encour-age the women to take time to complete the Work On It section at home. Draw attention to the "A to Z exercise" on page 91 (PG), and urge them to complete as much as they can on the handout.

spice it up

For extra fun, encourage the women to wear WHITE to group next week. Offer a prize for the most creatively dressed group member in white.

red hot tip

"I'm not sure if 'F' stands for Week Five or Fizzle Out. There's something about Week Five in many of our groups that causes women to give up. Don't be discouraged. This is the week I like to assign everyone to follow up with another group member during the week, send hand-written notes of blessing, or leave the group with a teaser they can't help but come back for. Week Six stands for SUCCESS!"

—*Julie Sanders, Knoxville, Tennessee*

Reflect On It

A self-review of your time after the session

- How did it go? Is there anything you wish you had done differently?
- What worked well?
- Spend time in prayer. Ask God to strengthen the faith of each woman, and reveal to her more about who He is and what He is able to do.
- Call or write group members who were absent. Ask if there is any way you can help or pray for them.
- Is there anyone who is currently in the midst of a fiery test or trial? Make a quick phone call, send an e-mail, or drop a "thinking of you" note in the mail.

red hot tip

"Ladies, You are CHOSEN! You are LOVED! You are BLESSED with all you need to do His work! His GRACE is with you as you lead."

—*Erin Leyen, Charlotte, North Carolina*

White Clothes to Wear

Overview: The church of Laodicea was known for its beautiful black wool, but Jesus said He had "white clothes for them to wear." In this week's lesson, we'll expose how easy it is to live "covered," hiding behind false labels and fear. Also, we will explore the freedom that is ours in Christ.

Prepare For It

Things to do before the session

- Prepare a schedule for your gathering. Read the Get Into It and Discuss It sections and choose the questions that will work best for your group.

- Watch Session 6 to familiarize yourself with the teaching.

- Handouts: The blank "Who I Am in Christ from A to Z" on page 58 (LG), and the completed "God's Attributes from A to Z" on page 59 (LG). Optional: poster board for a Get Into It activity.

- Pray for God to prepare hearts and minds as you tackle a sensitive subject.

- Send an uplifting e-mail and remind the women to wear WHITE to group, if they would like.

red hot tip

"Even when you feel your session is perfectly planned, the Holy Spirit may nudge you to do something different. Discern the voice you hear and if it is God, obey and be blessed."

—Kathy Bruins, Holland, Michigan

Get Into It

- Welcome everyone and open with prayer.

- Choose one of the Breaking the Ice exercises on page 95 (PG).

- Using a big piece of poster board, work together to record "God's Attributes from A to Z." Refer to Cindy's completed handout on page 57 (LG) as necessary. Ask, "Which attribute of God means the most to you? Explain."

- Have everyone open to page 94 of her Participant's Guide. Read the "New Garments" introduction from Cindy. Ask, "How do you connect with Cindy's gym class example? Can you relate?"

Watch It

Direct everyone to Watch It on page 96 (PG). Show the Session 6 video: "White Clothes to Wear."

Discuss It

● Facilitate the Discuss It questions beginning on page 99 (PG).

(((● Spice It Up: If time allows, watch Lifehouse's Everything Skit (search you-tube.com). It's a dramatic presentation of a woman leaving her "covered living" to experience Christ's radiance and unfailing love. (Encourage the women to watch it at home if you don't view it as a group.)

● Memory Verse (p. 98 PG): Ask a volunteer to look up this week's verse and read it aloud. Encourage the women to keep going on their memory verse work.

● Prayer Time: Using the prayer prompts as a guide, ask for a volunteer to close in prayer.

(((● Prayer Groups: Break into groups of four. Encourage the woman to write down on a piece of scrap paper the "false label" they wrestle with most often. After doing so, tell them to rip the paper up and place it in the garbage where those labels belong. Spend time in prayer, praying words of truth over one another. Remind the women that it is okay to "take a pass" on praying out loud.

Work On It

Pass out the blank "Who I Am in Christ from A to Z" handout (p. 58 LG). Draw attention to the "A to Z exercise" on page 108 (PG), and urge the women to complete as much as they can on the handout. Highlight the new nametag on page 108 (PG) and encourage the women to take time to complete the Work On It section at home.

spice it up

For extra fun, encourage the women to wear SUNGLASSES to group next week. Offer a prize for the snazziest sunglass-wearing group member.

red hot tip

"I pray God is teaching you mightily right now. Do not let Satan encourage you to lose your faith. Stay alert and turn to the One in whom you put your faith in the first place. He is worthy! He is the King of kings! He is FAITHFUL! There are just two more weeks to go. Ask God to encourage not only your own faithfulness, but also your group's."[6]

—*Beth Moore*

Reflect On It

A self-review of your time after the session

- How did it go? What worked well? Jot down three high points.

- Is there anything you wish you would have done differently?

- Spend time in prayer. Ask God to bear much kingdom fruit from the seeds that are being planted each week.

- Call or write group members who were absent. Remind them it's not the same without them at group, and ask if there is any way you can help fill them in on the material they missed.

- Is there anyone who was especially quiet? Didn't seem like her usual self? Send an e-mail or drop a "thinking of you" note in the mail.

red hot tip

"I'm so thankful you have been placed in this leadership role. You have the privilege of being used by the Lord to be a 'shame lifter' in the lives of your gals. You may even have some women who tell you their shame story for the very first time. What an honor!"

—*Marilyn Hontz*

SESSION 7

Receiving Sight

Overview: Jesus Christ came to give sight to the blind. In this week's lesson, we'll watch Christ in action as He helps the blind to see.

Prepare For It

Things to do before the session

- Read the Get Into It and Discuss It sections and choose the questions that should work best for your group.

- Watch Session 7 to familiarize yourself with the teaching.

- Handouts: The completed "Who I Am in Christ from A to Z." Optional: poster board for a Get Into It activity.

- Pray that God would open the eyes of each woman and that each of them would see Christ more clearly.

- Send an encouraging e-mail, especially after the sensitive subject of shame last week. Remind the women to bring their favorite sunglasses to group if they would like.

red hot tip

"Jesus knew each detail of what the Laodiceans needed to hear . . . about being 'gold' in the fire, needing 'eye salves' for their spiritual blindness, and exchanging 'white clothes' for their black wool. I am praying that you will also know God has planned out each detail of YOUR group . . . from each person in the group to each discussion that unfolds." —*Sara Roelofs, Grand Rapids, Michigan*

Get Into It

- Welcome everyone and open with prayer.
- (Choose one of the Breaking the Ice exercises on page 111 (PG).
- (((Using a big piece of poster board, work together to record "Who I Am in Christ from A to Z." Refer to Cindy's completed handout on page 59 (LG) as necessary. Ask, "Which truth means the most to you? Explain."
- Have everyone open to page 110 of her Participant's Guide. Read the "Coincidence?" introduction from Cindy.

Watch It

Direct everyone to Watch It on page 112 (PG). Show the Session 7 video: "Receiving Sight."

Discuss It

- Facilitate the Discuss It questions beginning on page 116 (PG).
- ((Blind spots—we all have them. If time allows, discuss No. 3 from the Work On It section on page 122 (PG). Read the opening statement aloud. Go around the group discussing ways the list could cause one to have a blind spot, or "no light perception."

(((● Spend time discussing "when the lights came on" for each woman (see No. 4 on page 117 PG). Thank God for helping your blind eyes see. Sing the song "Amazing Grace" together. (Print the words from an online source, or find the song on youtube.com with lyrics printed.)

● Memory Verse (p. 115 PG): This week you'll be memorizing Psalm 34:8. Cheer the women on as they continue their memory verse challenge.

● Prayer Time: Using the prayer prompts as a guide, ask for a volunteer to close in prayer.

(((● Prayer Groups: Break into groups of four. Write down names or initials of men, women, and children the women know who are living in spiritual blindness. Spend time praying for God to open their eyes and to reveal himself to each one. Remind the women that it is okay to "take a pass" on praying out loud.

Work On It

Encourage the women to take time to complete the Work On It section at home. Remind them not to miss the blind spots exercise on page 122 (PG).

Faith Journey

Your group has had the opportunity to hear Cindy share her faith journey through the video teachings. Now it's your turn! Give each member a sheet of paper and ask each woman to make a graph of her faith journey. Instruct members to note the high points and low points of their lives and to recall what was happening during those periods. Encourage everyone to include the time when they accepted Christ into their life. Invite those who are willing to explain their graphs to the group in the coming weeks.[7]

Note: You may want to have the women complete this at home, or if time allows, you may want to give the women a chance to start it during your group session. Also, dear facilitator, you may want to complete your Faith Journey and have it available as a sample when you share this exercise.

red hot tip

"Sometimes you walk away from your small group time asking 'what just happened?' It didn't go as expected or planned and you are wondering what about all that time spent praying and preparing. You are not alone. We have all been there. Trust that God knew exactly how this would go, trust that He will use the time spent praying and preparing for your good and for the greater good of your group, maybe not today but He will use it." —*Amy Hodgkinson, Walker, Michigan*

Reflect On It

A self-review of your time after the session

- How did it go? Did you have a favorite moment?
- Spend time in prayer. Ask God to reveal to each woman any blind spots in her life. Pray that her spiritual eyes would be opened.
- Call or write group members who were absent. Let them know they were missed. Encourage them to come to the Week 8 session.
- Is there anyone who has been vulnerable in your group discussion time? Send her a quick e-mail to acknowledge her openness and thank her for being "real."

red hot tip

"Question: Who is praying for you this week as you prepare for the final session? Write her name here: _____ Call her and ask her to pray with you. It will feed your soul as Jesus intercedes with the two of you!" —*April Garretson, Christiansburg, Virginia*

The Red Hot Faith Backpack

Overview: This week we will review and reflect on the important life lessons we've learned from the church of Laodicea.

Prepare For It

Things to do before the session

- Prepare a schedule for your gathering. Read the Get Into It and Discuss It sections and choose the questions that will work best for your group.

- Watch Session 8 to familiarize yourself with the teaching.

- Pray for God to give the women the strength, faith, and tenacity to finish this Bible study well.

- Send a reminder e-mail and let all the women know you are praying for them!

  Note: If you are **not** having a *Red Hot Faith* Fiesta, you may want to peek at the Fiesta ideas and incorporate them into your Session 8 gathering. Let the women know how proud you are of their hard work. Celebrate their commitment to living with Red Hot Faith.

- **Note:** If you **are** hosting a *Red Hot Faith* Fiesta, read through the ideas on pages 50–53 (LG). Jot down celebration ideas to discuss with the group, make a list of preparation needs, and have signup sheets available to distribute at the end of the group session.

red hot tip

"You're nearing the finish! You have done great work, and God is using you to touch the lives of the women in your group. Press on as you finish these last couple weeks, and know that God is working through you!" —Laura Kuperus, Grand Rapids, Michigan

Get Into It

- Welcome everyone and open with prayer.
- Choose one of the Breaking the Ice exercises on page 127 (PG).
- After completing one of the Breaking the Ice exercises, divide the women up into pairs. Ask participants to talk with a partner for 2 to 3 minutes about one thing that has stood out to them from this *Red Hot Faith* study. *Option:* When you come back together, ask for a few volunteers to share with the larger group what they discussed.
- Have everyone open to page 126 of her Participant's Guide. Read the "Packing Up" introduction from Cindy.

Watch It

Direct everyone to Watch It on page 128 (PG). Show the Session 8 video: "The Red Hot Faith Backpack."

Discuss It

● Facilitate the Discuss It questions beginning on page 131 (PG).

(((● Ask the women to write on a piece of paper her answer to Discuss It No. 2, along with her name and e-mail address. Trade the paper with a partner, and commit to praying and encouraging one another.

● Memory Verse (p. 130 PG): Facilitator, do you have a story of how the Scripture memory has had an impact on you? Share with the women, and ask them to share which verse has affected them the most, and in what ways.

(((● Memory Verse: Review the verses you've learned. You may want to read them aloud, leaving out key words, while the women fill in the blanks. Here's the Week 1 verse as an example:

"How great is the _____ the Father has _____ on us, that we should be called the _____ of God! And that is _____ _____ _____!" —1 John 3:1

● Prayer Time: Using the prayer prompts as a guide, ask for a volunteer to close in prayer.

(((● Prayer Groups: Break into groups of four. Invite the women to share personal prayer requests, and then pray for one another using the prayer prompts on page 132 (PG), as well as praying as they feel comfortable. Remind the women that it is okay to "take a pass" on praying out loud if they'd prefer.

Work On It

Encourage the women to take time to complete the Work On It section at home. Remind them to bring their Participant's Guide back for the Fiesta.

Coming Up next week

We celebrate! Encourage all members to come back next week to celebrate the end of a "job well done." How will you celebrate your completion of *Red Hot Faith*? Discuss Fiesta details and distribute sign-up sheets, as needed. Just for fun, consider wearing red to the fiesta.

spice it up

If this is your last group session, don't forget to take a quick "after" photo of your group and e-mail it to cindy@cindybultema.com. Share some of your group highlights too.

red hot tip

"I asked the group of Bible study girls, 'What do you do when a study is over?' Their collective answer: 'Wait for the next one to start.' On the last day, be sure to give some guidance and exhortation about spending time in the Word, having a plan for staying engaged with God, and being faithful to redeem the 'in-between' times."

—*Julie Sanders, Knoxville, TN*

Reflect On It

A self-review of your time after the session

- Spend time in prayer. Ask God to seal the work He has accomplished in each of the women's lives.

- Call or write group members who were absent. Let them know they were missed. Invite them to the Red Hot Faith Fiesta, and share ways they can help.

- Is there anyone who you sense could use a word of encouragement? Why not "be cold" and send an e-mail or drop a "thinking of you" note in the mail.

red hot tip

"Hopefully, the ladies in your group have caught the vision of being His witness on their trade routes every day. I encourage you to commission them to take a deeper step in reaching out by praying about facilitating a *Red Hot Faith* study in their home or workplace. A few of the women may want to team up and form a group by prayerfully extending an invitation to women along their trade routes. Who knows what God may have next!"

—Julie Richardson, Grand Rapids, Michigan

BONUS SESSION

Red Hot Faith Fiesta

Prepare For It

Things to do before the session

- Pray for God's leading and guidance as you prepare a fun, celebratory last group session.

- Decorations: Consider using the "red hot" theme. Ideas include Red Hot™ candies, red paper products, etc. Another option: a chili pepper theme. Look for discounted Cinco de Mayo paper products (especially chili pepper confetti ☺). Is there a gifted party planner and/or decorator in your group? Ask for her help.

- Photographer: Recruit a group member to photograph your fun gathering.

- Refreshments: Keep it simple and have a chips and salsa bar (with a healthy option too). Or pass around a sign-up and have everyone bring their favorite festive dish. Check Cindy's website for a variety of fun spicy recipes. Don't forget drink choices. You may want to provide something steaming hot, something ice cold, but nothing lukewarm!

- Send an e-mail with Fiesta details. Remind the women to wear red for fun.

- Prepare a schedule based on the needs and personality of your group. See below for a few ideas:

❨ 60-minute Group	❨❨ 90-minute Group	❨❨❨ 120-minute Group
Get Into It (10 minutes) • Welcome • Yea, God! Yea, you! • Prayer	**Get Into It** (10 minutes) • Welcome • Yea, God! Yea, you! • Prayer	**Get Into It** (10 minutes) • Welcome • Yea, God! Yea, you! • Prayer
Enjoy It (15 minutes) Food & Fellowship	**Enjoy It** (30 minutes) Food & Fellowship	**Enjoy It** (30 minutes) Food & Fellowship
Share It (30 minutes)	**Share It** (50 minutes)	**Share It** (40 minutes)
Wrap It Up (10 minutes) • Coming up next • Closing Prayer	**Wrap It Up** (10 minutes) • Coming up next • Closing Prayer	**Prayer Groups** (20 minutes) **Wrap It Up** (10 minutes) • Coming up next • Closing Prayer

Get Into It

- Welcome everyone to the *Red Hot Faith* Fiesta!
- Share a few heartfelt words about what you have enjoyed as the facilitator of this group.
- Yea, God! Yea, you! Thank God for His leading and guidance. Spend time honoring the women for their faithful commitment.
- Pray. Thank God for His presence and ask for His blessing over your group.

Enjoy It

Spend time fellowshiping and enjoying the snacks. If you sense your group may need more structured social time, consider:

- Index cards with conversation starters on the table.
- Google "small-group icebreakers" and find a simple idea.
- Share favorite "red hot" recipes.
- Begin the Share It exercises as soon as everyone has refreshments.

Share It

- Facilitate the Work On It questions beginning on page 133 (PG).

- Woo-Hoo Awards: Give verbal or fun homemade awards to each group member for faith-filled victories or new relationships formed on their trade routes. (See page 11 LG for "Just for Fun" ideas).

(((● "Red Hot" seat: Have an individual sit on a chair in the center of the room and ask each group member to take a few moments and express appreciation for that person. It can be as simple as asking everyone to finish, "What I appreciate about you is . . . ," or, "You are important to our group because . . ." Or you can give everyone a few minutes to speak freely from her heart to honor this person. After the last person has spoken, give the honoree a standing ovation.[8]

(((● Faith journeys: Ask for volunteers to share their faith journey. See page 43 in this guide for more details.

(((● Say, "We've spent the past eight weeks unpacking Revelation 3:14–22, a letter with a personal message from Jesus to the church in Laodicea and His followers everywhere. Now it is your turn to write a letter to Him." Distribute paper and envelopes to each woman. Play quiet music and give each woman 10 to 15 minutes to write her thoughts on paper. Invite each to tuck the letter in her Bible for safe-keeping.

- Memory Verse: Does anyone know all eight verses? Ask for volunteers to recite them aloud, and consider giving fun awards to anyone who has completed the Memory Verse Challenge. Cheer for all the women for any progress they have made!

(((● Prayer Groups: Break into groups of four. Invite the women to share personal prayer requests, and then pray for one another. Remind the women that it is okay to "take a pass" on praying out loud.

Wrap It Up

- Looking Ahead: Is there a new group starting? Share upcoming details, or confirm contact info for more communication in the future.

- Prayer Time: Gather in a circle. If comfortable, ask the women to join hands. Spend time in prayer thanking God for the insights, lessons, and truth learned, as well as the new relationships formed.

- Sing About It: Consider closing with a song as a benediction. "My Friends, May You Grow in Grace" is a personal favorite. Search youtube.com for the song lyrics and melody, or choose a favorite of your own.

- Spice It Up: Don't forget to take a quick "after" photo of your group and e-mail it to cindy@cindybultema.com. Share some of your fiesta photos too.

Reflect On It

A self-review of your time after the session

- Spend time in prayer. Pray that the women would not merely listen to the Word but that they would also do what it says (James 1:22). Pray that they would continue to look for ways to put their Red Hot Faith into action.

- We would love to hear how this study has been an encouragement to you and the women in your group. Visit Cindy's website at www.cindybultema.com or e-mail at cindy@cindybultema.com to share how this study has had an impact on you. Please invite everyone in your group to do the same. Cindy can't wait to hear from you!

Welcome to *Red Hot Faith!*

Our Purpose and Desire: We believe God is raising up a group of women, worshiping the One true God, living out lives of complete surrender to Christ and His call for their lives, and courageously walking in the truth.

Our Commitment:

- Grow closer to Jesus
- Give and receive unconditional love and acceptance
- Be open, vulnerable, and real
- Practice complete confidentiality
- Study the Bible together
- Be encouraged and inspired
- Make new friendships
- Spend time in prayer for one another
- Have fun!

Overview: Our Bible study will meet every Monday evening September 9 until November 4 from 7:00 p.m. to 8:30 p.m. in the Sunshine Room.

General Evening Schedule

7:00 – 7:15 Opening (Welcome, announcements, group activities)
7:15 – 7:45 Video Teaching
7:45 – 8:30 Small Groups (Discussion, Bible exploration, prayer)

Snacks: Food and fellowship are always a good mix! Please feel no pressure to bring something, but if you'd like to share a goodie, let us know!

Prayer: Your small-group leader will always be able to pray with you, in group or throughout the week.

Red Hot Faith Icebreaker

🔄 **Recent vacation?** _____

🔄 **Early morning or late-night person?** _____

🔄 **Dog or pets' names?** _____

🔄 **How many in your family?**_____

🔄 **Occupation?**_____

🔄 **Thankful for?** _____

🔄 **Favorite movie/book?** _____

🔄 **Are you a summer or winter lover?** _____

🔄 **Is this your first time in a small group?** _____

🔄 **Tired of . . .?**_____

🔄 **Happiest when?** _____

Thanks to my friends at Woodside Bible Church of White Lake, Michigan, for sharing their fun RHF icebreaker.

God's Attributes from A to Z

A _____

B _____

C _____

D _____

E _____

F _____

G _____

H _____

I _____

J _____

K _____

L _____

M _____

N _____

O _____

P _____

Q _____

R _____

S _____

T _____

U _____

V _____

W _____

X _____

Y _____

Z _____

God's Attributes from A to Z

A Advocate (Job 16:19) _____

B Burden Bearer (Psalm 68:19) _____

C Comforter in Sorrow (Jeremiah 8:18) _____

D Deliverer (Psalm 70:5) _____

E Eternal God (Deuteronomy 33:27) _____

F Forgiving God (Nehemiah 9:17) _____

G Guide (Psalm 48:14) _____

H Healer (Exodus 15:26) _____

I I AM (Exodus 3:14) _____

J Just and Mighty One (Job 34:17) _____

K King of Kings (Revelation 19:16) _____

L Light (Psalm 27:1) _____

M Most High (Genesis 14:18–22) _____

N Name above all Names (Psalm 99:3) _____

O Our Dwelling Place (Psalm 90:1) _____

P Patient God (2 Peter 3:9) _____

Q Quieter with Love (Zephaniah 3:17) _____

R Rock and Refuge (Psalm 62:7) _____

S Strong Tower (Proverbs 18:10) _____

T Truth Teller (Isaiah 45:19) _____

U Understanding (Isaiah 11:2) _____

V Victorious (Psalm 60:12) _____

W Wonderful Counselor (Isaiah 9:6) _____

X eXalted One (Psalm 99:2) _____

Y Your Glory (Psalm 57:11) _____

Z Zealous for Your Holy Name (Ezekiel 39:25) _____

Who I Am in Christ
from A to Z

A _____

B _____

C _____

D _____

E _____

F _____

G _____

H _____

I _____

J _____

K _____

L _____

M _____

N _____

O _____

P _____

Q _____

R _____

S _____

T _____

U _____

V _____

W _____

X _____

Y _____

Z _____

Who I Am in Christ from A to Z

A Accepted (Romans 15:7)

B Beautiful (Psalm 45:11)

C Chosen (1 Peter 2:9)

D Delivered (Psalm 116:8)

E Equipped (2 Timothy 3:17)

F Free (Galatians 5:1)

G Gifted (Romans 12:6)

H Holy (Ephesians 1:4)

I Instrument of Righteousness (Romans 6:13)

J Justified (Romans 5:1)

K Known by God (1 Corinthians 8:3)

L Light (Ephesians 5:8–9)

M More Than a Conqueror (Romans 8:37)

N New Creation (2 Corinthians 5:17)

O Overcomer (1 John 5:4,5)

P Peace-filled (John 14:27)

Q Qualified to Share Inheritance (Colossians 1:12)

R Redeemed (Ephesians 1:7)

S Sealed (Ephesians 4:30)

T Temple of God (1 Corinthians 6:19)

U United with Christ (Romans 6:5)

V Victorious (1 Corinthians 15:57)

W Workmanship (Ephesians 2:10)

X eXtremely Loved (1 John 3:1)

Y Yoked with Christ (Matthew 11:29–30)

Z Zealous (Romans 12:11)

Trade Route Example

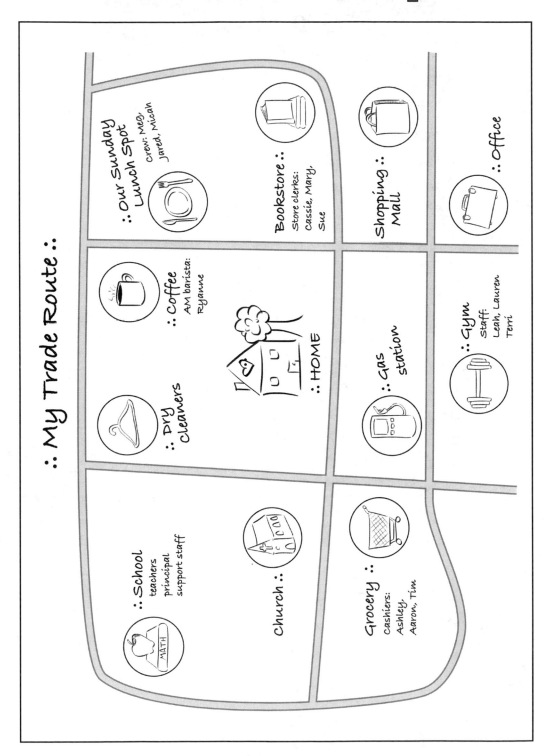

:: My Trade Route ::

:: Our Sunday Lunch Spot
crew: Meg, Jared, Micah

Bookstore ::
Store clerks:
Cassie, Mary,
Sue

Shopping ::
Mall

:: Office

:: Coffee
AM barista:
Ryanne

:: Dry
Cleaners

:: HOME

:: Gas
station

:: Gym
staff:
Leah, Lauren
Terri

:: School
teachers
principal
support staff

Church ::

Grocery ::
cashiers:
Ashley,
Aaron, Tim

Notes

1. Lively, Amy. *The Neighborhood Cafe Planning Guide.* 2012, 11.
2. Smith, Allie Marie. *Becoming Who You Are in Christ.* Loveland: Group, 2012, 85.
3. Lively, 45.
4. Moore, Beth. *Living Beyond Yourself Leader's Guide.* Nashville: Lifeway Christian Resources, 2004, 8.
5. Moore, 10.
6. Moore, 15.
7. Moore, Beth. *Believing God: Leader Guide.* Nashville, TN: LifeWay, 2002, 17.
8. Gladen, Steve. *Leading Small Groups with Purpose: Everything You Need to Lead a Healthy Group.* Grand Rapids, MI: Baker, 2012, 103.